# No Backbone!
## The World of Invertebrates

# Bloodsucking Leeches

by Pearl Neuman

Consultants:

Dr. John W. Reynolds
Oligochaetology Laboratory
Kitchener, Ontario, Canada

Patricia S. Sadeghian
Associate Curator of Invertebrate Zoology
Santa Barbara Museum of Natural History

BEARPORT
PUBLISHING

NEW YORK, NEW YORK

**Credits**

Cover, © A.N.T. Photo Library/NHPA and © Hugh Lansdown/FLPA; TOC, © Pavlenko Evgeniy/Shutterstock; 4, © Hugh Lansdown/
FLPA; 5, © Brian Bevan/Ardea; 6T, © Willem Kolvoort/Nature Picture Library; 6B, © Kurt G/Shutterstock; 7, © Timothy Branning;
8, © A.N.T. Photo Library/NHPA/Photoshot; 9, © Jurgen Otto/A.N.T. Photo Library; 10T, © blickwinkel/Hecker/Sauer/Still Pictures;
10B, © BIOS/Peter Arnold Inc.; 11, © Hecker/Sauer/Still Pictures; 12T, © Robert & Linda Mitchell; 12B, © A.N.T. Photo Library/NHPA;
13, © Martin Dohrn/Spl/Photolibrary; 14-15, © Dwight Kuhn/Dwight Kuhn Photography; 16T, © Dwight Kuhn/Dwight Kuhn
Photography; 16B, © Mark MacEwen/Photolibrary; 17, © Geoff Tompkinson/Science Photo Library; 18, © The Granger Collection,
New York; 19, © Jean-Loup Charmet/Science Photo Library; 20-21, © Ian Cook/Time Life Pictures/Getty Images; 22TL, © Phil
Degginger/Alamy; 22TR, © Mary Beth Angelo/Photo Researchers, Inc.; 22BL, © Biosphoto/Guihard Claude; 22BR, © Marevision/
age fotostock/Photolibrary; 22Spot, © Mircea Bezergheanu/Shutterstock; 23TL, © Jim Wehtje/Photodisc/Getty Images; 23TR,
© Mark MacEwen/Photolibrary; 23BL, © Kurt G/Shutterstock; 23BR, © Willem Kolvoort/Nature Picture Library; 24, © Mircea
Bezergheanu/Shutterstock.

Publisher: Kenn Goin
Editorial Director: Adam Siegel
Creative Director: Spencer Brinker
Original Design: Dawn Beard Creative
Photo Researcher: Q2A Media: Poulomi Basu

*Library of Congress Cataloging-in-Publication Data*

Neuman, Pearl.
Bloodsucking leeches / by Pearl Neuman.
  p. cm. — (No backbone! The world of invertebrates)
Includes bibliographical references and index.
ISBN-13: 978-1-59716-755-0 (library binding)
ISBN-10: 1-59716-755-X (library binding)
1. Leeches—Juvenile literature. I. Title.
QL391.A6N48 2009
592'.66--dc22

2008040612

For more information, write to Bearport Publishing Company, Inc., 101 Fifth Avenue, Suite 6R,
New York, New York 10003. Printed in the United States of America.

10 9 8 7 6 5 4 3 2 1

# Contents

# Bloodsuckers

Leeches are worms that live in swamps, ponds, and other watery places.

Some leeches eat tiny fish and snails.

Most leeches, however, get their food in a different way.

They suck blood from animals—including people!

Leeches can be found all over the world. Some even live on land—in places such as warm, wet forests.

leech in a rain forest

# Many Sizes, Many Colors

There are more than 650 kinds of leeches.

Some are less than half an inch (1 cm) long.

Others stretch out to 12 inches (30 cm) or more.

The largest leech in the world is the Amazon leech.

It can grow up to 18 inches (46 cm) in length.

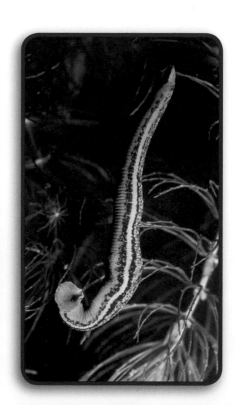

Many leeches are black or brown. Some, however, are very colorful with bright stripes or spots.

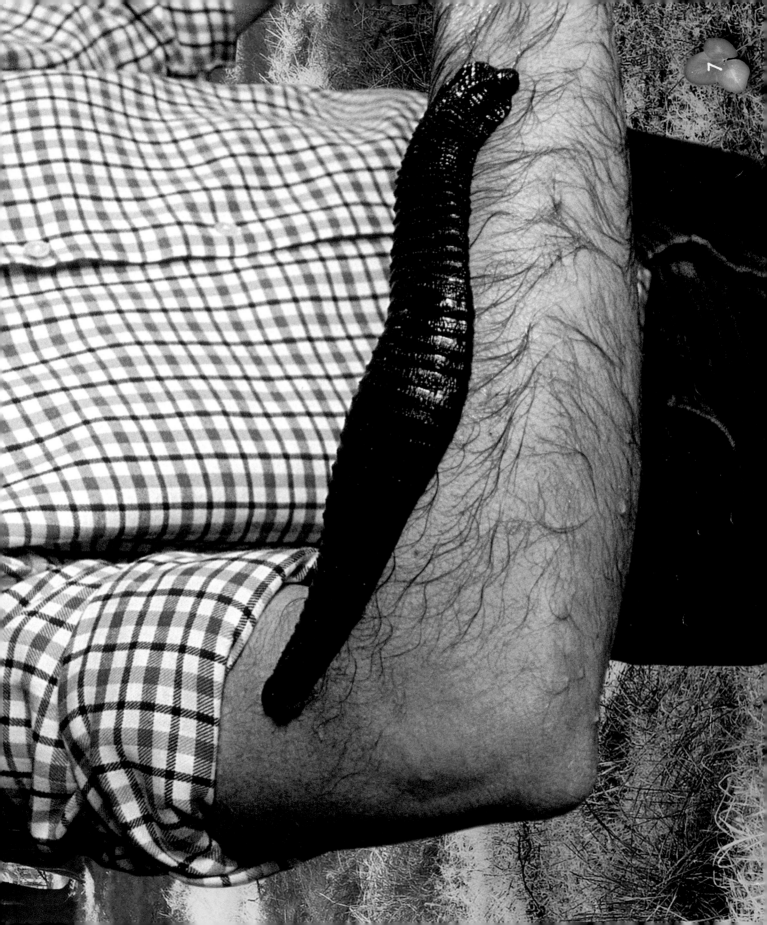

# Many Segments

All leeches have a body made up of 34 **segments**, or parts.

The segments look like rings around the leech's body.

Most leeches have a small **sucker** under the head segment and a larger sucker at the tail.

A leech uses its head and tail suckers to move from place to place like an inchworm.

It also uses them to feed.

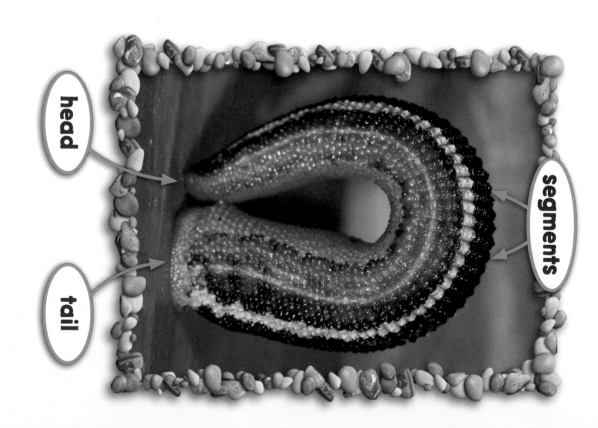

head

tail

segments

head sucker

tail sucker

A leech has a large stomach inside its body. The stomach is between the head sucker and the tail sucker.

# Out for Blood

Bloodsucking leeches can sense when food is nearby.

They have two to ten tiny eyes on their head that help them find food.

They also have special body parts in their segments that can sense movement and changes in light.

When a victim comes close, a leech uses its tail sucker to grab on to the animal's skin.

Then the leech attaches its head sucker to the victim—and bites.

leech

newt

leech

frog

Leeches feed on the blood of almost any animal they find in the water, including fish, frogs, turtles, birds, and humans.

leech

# Having a Bite

When a leech bites, it cuts through an animal's skin with its sharp teeth.

It also puts a liquid into the bite that stops the victim from feeling pain.

Since the animal does not feel the bloodsucking worm's bite, it does not try to get the leech off its body.

The leech sucks until it is full of blood.

Then it drops off its victim and rests.

A leech swallows up to five times its weight in blood. Its stomach stretches to store the blood.

stomach filled with blood

# Eat or Be Eaten

Leeches don't just feed off other animals.

They are also food for other animals.

Some insects, such as beetles, eat leeches.

Ducks, turtles, and fish eat leeches, too.

Some leeches eat other leeches.

# Little Leeches

Like all leeches, bloodsucking leeches lay eggs.

To protect the eggs, leeches make soft **cocoons** filled with fluid.

Baby leeches hatch inside the cocoons.

For a few weeks, they feed on the fluid around them.

Then they leave the cocoons and start feeding on blood.

cocoon

eggs

Baby leeches look like tiny adults.

baby leech leaving cocoon

# A Bloody Past

Hundreds of years ago, doctors used leeches to try to cure the sick.

They thought that many illnesses were caused by "bad blood" in a person's body.

They placed leeches on sick people to remove some of the blood.

Usually, however, the sick person just got weaker.

Over time, most doctors stopped using leeches in their work.

Using leeches to suck a sick person's blood is called bloodletting.

**bloodletting**

# Saving Lives

In 1985, a doctor in Boston tried using leeches in a new way.

He placed them on a boy's ear to get blood flowing after an operation.

This time, the treatment worked.

The boy got better.

Since then, many other doctors have used bloodsucking leeches to help heal people.

The bloodsuckers are now lifesavers!

# A World of Invertebrates

An animal that has a skeleton with a **backbone** inside its body is a *vertebrate* (VUR-tuh-brit). Mammals, birds, fish, reptiles, and amphibians are all vertebrates.

An animal that does not have a skeleton with a backbone inside its body is an *invertebrate* (in-VUR-tuh-brit). More than 95 percent of all kinds of animals on Earth are invertebrates.

Some invertebrates, such as insects and spiders, have hard skeletons—called exoskeletons—on the outside of their bodies. Other invertebrates, such as worms and jellyfish, have soft, squishy bodies with no exoskeletons to protect them.

Here are four worms that are related to leeches. Like leeches, they are all invertebrates.

**Sandworm**

**Tube Worm**

**Earthworm**

**Bristleworm**

# Glossary

**backbone**
(BAK-bohn)
a group of
connected bones
that run along
the backs of some
animals, such as
dogs, birds, and fish;
also called a spine

**segments**
(SEG-muhnts)
ring-like parts of a
worm's body

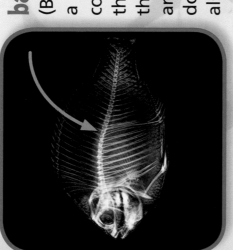

**cocoons**
(kuh-KOONZ)
containers that
leeches make to
protect their eggs
until they hatch

**sucker**
(SUHK-ur)
a round part at
each end of a
leech's body used
for sucking and
holding on to
something

# Index

# Read More

**Kite, L. Patricia.** *Leeches.* Minneapolis, MN: Lerner (2005).

**Somervill, Barbara A.** *Leeches: Waiting in the Water.* New York: PowerKids Press (2008).

**Wyborny, Sheila.** *Leeches.* Farmington Hills, MI: KidHaven Press (2005).

# Learn More Online

To learn more about leeches, visit

www.bearportpublishing.com/NoBackbone-CreepyCrawlers

# About the Author

Pearl Neuman lives in Bergen County, New Jersey.
She does her best to avoid leeches and other bloodsuckers.